What's in this book

学习内容 Contents 2

读一读 Read 4

听听说说 Listen and say 12

写一写 Write 16

多元学习 Connections 18

温习 Checkpoint 20

分享 Sharing 22

This book belongs to

_____

方向 The directions

学习内容 Contents

沟通 Communication

说出交通工具
Say means of transport

说出方向
Say the directions

生词 New words

★ 东	east
★ 南	south
★ 西	west
★ 北	north
★ 远	far
★ 近	near
★ 校车	school bus
★ 出租车	taxi
★ 更	even more
★ 要	will

Post Office

School

Supermarket

公里	kilometre (km)
公共汽车	bus
电车	tram
语文	language
考试	examination

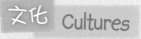 文化 Cultures

中国古代四大发明之指南针
One of the Four Great Inventions
of ancient China——the compass

句式 Sentence patterns

坐公共汽车或电车更快。
It is faster to take the bus or the tram.

浩浩和玲玲要坐校车回家。
Hao Hao and Ling Ling will take the
school bus to go home.

 跨学科学习 Project

制作指南针，并利用指南
针辨认方向
Make a compass and use it
to tell directions

Get ready

1 Have you ever been lost somewhere before?

2 What did you do to find your way?

3 How can you tell that the boy in the picture is lost?

xiào chē
校车

yào
要

School bus

浩浩和玲玲要坐校车回家。在车站，一个男孩迷路了，向他们问路。

"你们好，请问语文中心怎么走？"
男孩问。

dōng
东

nán
南

gōng lǐ
公里

gōng gòng qì chē
公共汽车

diàn chē
电车

gèng
更

"语文中心在东南方向，要走两公里。坐公共汽车或电车更快。"浩浩说。

"这么远啊，我以为很近。我要去考试，怎么去最快？"男孩问。

"坐出租车最快。西边有一个出租车站。"玲玲说。

"直走到路口，向北转就到车站了。"
玲玲说。"谢谢你们！"男孩说。

Let's think

1 Recall the story and circle the correct answers.

1 男孩要去哪里？

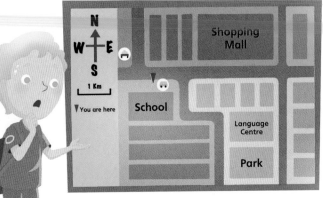

2 坐什么车去最快？

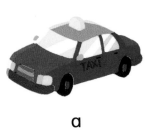

a

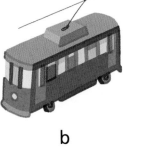

b

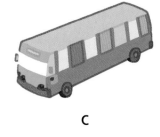

c

2 What would you do if you got lost? Tick the boxes and discuss with your friend.

New words

 1 Learn the new words.

电车

校车

公共汽车

出租车

更快

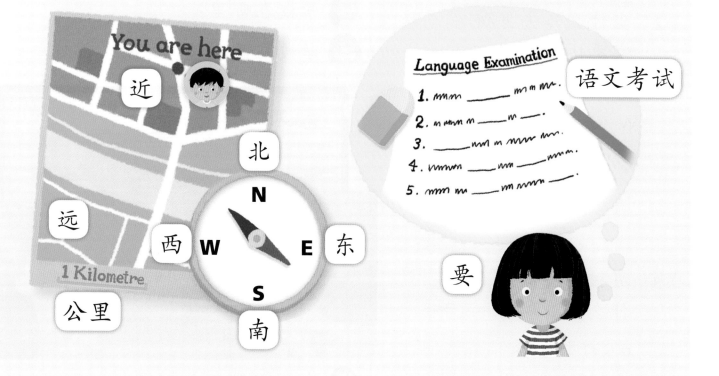

You are here

近

北

远

西 W

东 E

公里

南

语文考试

要

2 Say the words to your friend and ask him/her to point out the correct words above.

1 Listen and circle the correct letters.

 2 Look at the pictures. Listen to the story a

1 动物园在学校的
哪个方向？
a 南边
b 西边
c 北边

①

学校在哪里？

学校在西北边。

2 坐什么车去男孩
家更快？
a 公共汽车
b 电车
c 出租车

③

3 男孩要去做
什么？
a 打羽毛球
b 考试
c 看书

公共汽车站在哪里？

路上有汽车和校车，但是没有看
到公共汽车站。

哪里可以骑自行车？

东南面的草地边可以骑自行车。

小狗要去哪里？

小狗要去草地上玩，很近。

3 Write the letters and say.

> a 公共汽车　　b 东　　c 更
> d 西　　　　　e 远　　f 要

1

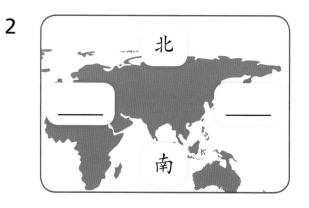

弟弟比我矮，妹妹比我＿＿矮。

2

北

南

3

我们＿＿坐＿＿去爷爷家。

爷爷家很＿＿。

Task

How do your classmates go to school every day? Make a transport survey chart and report.

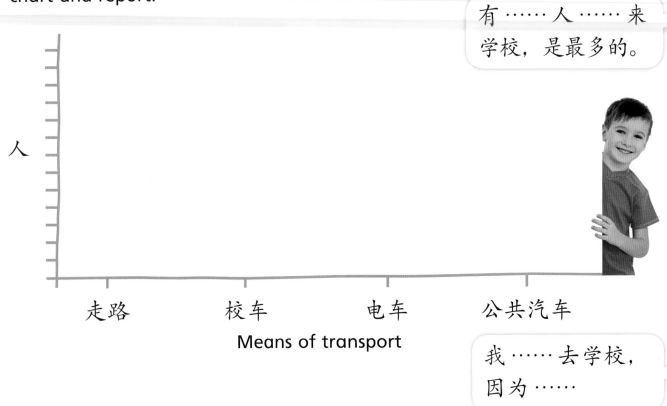

人

走路　　　校车　　　电车　　　公共汽车

Means of transport

有……人……来学校，是最多的。

我……去学校，因为……

Game

Match the halves of the means of transport together and then find the correct word for each one.

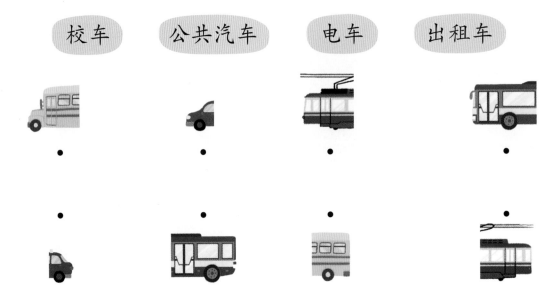

校车　　　公共汽车　　　电车　　　出租车

Chant

北

西

东

南

我要从东走到西，
我要从南走到北，
我要去不同的城市，
我要去很远的地方。

我要从西走到东，
我要从北走到南，
我要去不同的国家，
我要去更远的地方。

生活用语 Daily expressions

去……怎么走？
How can I get to …?

不远。
Not far away.

1 Trace and write the characters.

一 二 亍 元 元 远 远

远 远 远

一 厂 斤 斤 近 近

近 近 近

一 亍 币 币 西 西 覀 要 要

要 要 要

2 Write and say.

石头很＿＿，
船很＿＿。

校车＿＿开了，
请快点上车。

3 Fill in the blanks with the correct words. Colour the shells using the same colours.

我们　远　近　天　家人

今年夏＿＿＿，我和＿＿＿＿一起坐汽车去海边的城市旅行。那里在我们家的东边，很＿＿＿，＿＿＿＿坐车用了两个小时。城市的北边还有动物园，坐车只用二十分钟，很＿＿＿。＿＿＿＿都玩得很开心。

拼音输入法 Pinyin input

Match the sentences to the pictures using the letters and then organize the sentences into a meaningful paragraph. Type it out.

☐　　　☐　　　☐　　　☐

a　大象还很喜欢玩水。它们真可爱。

b　大象的耳朵很大，鼻子很长。

c　我最喜欢的动物是大象。三岁时，我和爸爸一起去动物园看大象。

d　它喜欢吃草。

Cultures

1 Did you know that the compass was one of the Four Great Inventions of ancient China? Learn about it.

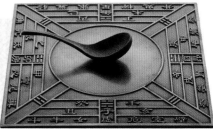

This compass was made up of a bronze plate and a magnetized spoon. It was used to identify directions and tell fortunes in ancient China.

This compass was used for navigation during the 11th century. The magnetized needle could move freely and point to the earth's magnetic poles.

The ancient Chinese compasses pointed to the south. Today's compasses, however, point to the north

2 Where are the stations? Talk about them with your friend.

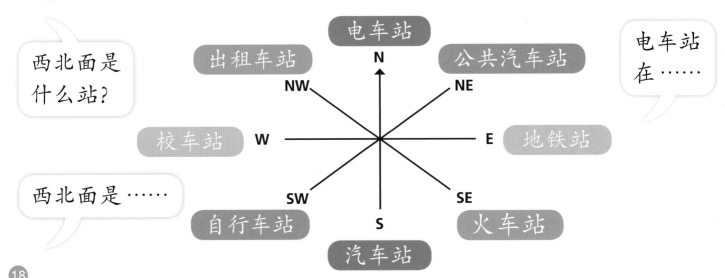

西北面是什么站?

西北面是……

电车站在……

18

Project

1 Make a compass.

Observe the sun or stars to find out which direction is north and mark on your compass!

2 Use the compass to identify the positions of your home, nearby buildings and the school. Discuss with your friend.

学校在……边，
公共汽车站在学
校的……边。

我家在城市
的……面，
我……上学。

我家在学校的……边，
不远，向……走一公里。

1 Answer the questions to help the children find the way to their destinations

1 这是什么车？它向什么方向开？

2  请问语文中心怎么走？

3 大卫家门口有什么车站？

4 大卫家到花园有十公里，很 ⬜ 。

5 去大卫家，坐电车还是公共汽车更快？

6 活动中心在什么方向？我 ⬜ 去那里和同学们一起打球。

2 Work with your friend. Colour the stars and the chillies.

Words	说	读	写
东	☆	☆	🌶
南	☆	☆	🌶
西	☆	☆	🌶
北	☆	☆	🌶
远	☆	☆	☆
近	☆	☆	☆
校车	☆	☆	🌶
出租车	☆	☆	🌶
更	☆	☆	🌶
要	☆	☆	☆
公里	☆	🌶	🌶

Words and sentences	说	读	写
公共汽车	☆	🌶	🌶
电车	☆	🌶	🌶
语文	☆	🌶	🌶
考试	☆	🌶	🌶
坐公共汽车或电车更快。	☆	☆	🌶
浩浩和玲玲要坐校车回家。	☆	☆	🌶

Say means of transport	☆
Say the directions	☆

3 What does your teacher say?

My teacher says ...

分享 Sharing

Words I remember

东	dōng	east
南	nán	south
西	xī	west
北	běi	north
远	yuǎn	far
近	jìn	near
校车	xiào chē	school bus
出租车	chū zū chē	taxi
更	gèng	even more
要	yào	will
公里	gōng lǐ	kilometre (km)
公共汽车	gōng gòng qì chē	bus
电车	diàn chē	tram

Post Office

School

Supermarket

语文	yǔ wén	language
考试	kǎo shì	examination

Other words

车站	chē zhàn	station
迷路	mí lù	to lose one's way
向	xiàng	toward
中心	zhōng xīn	center
方向	fāng xiàng	direction
以为	yǐ wéi	to presume, to think
直	zhí	straight
路口	lù kǒu	intersection
转	zhuǎn	to turn
就	jiù	just

OXFORD
UNIVERSITY PRESS

Oxford University Press is a department of the University of Oxford.
It furthers the University's objective of excellence in research, scholarship,
and education by publishing worldwide. Oxford is a registered trade mark of
Oxford University Press in the UK and in certain other countries

Published in Hong Kong by
Oxford University Press (China) Limited
39th Floor, One Kowloon, 1 Wang Yuen Street, Kowloon Bay,
Hong Kong

Illustrated by Anne Lee, Emily Chan, KY Chan and Wildman

Photographs for reproduction permitted by Dreamstime.com

China National Publications Import & Export (Group) Corporation is an authorized distributor of
Oxford Elementary Chinese.

Please contact content@cnpiec.com.cn or 86-10-65856782

ISBN: 978-0-19-047010-4

10 9 8 7 6 5 4 3 2